Zip Zap Man

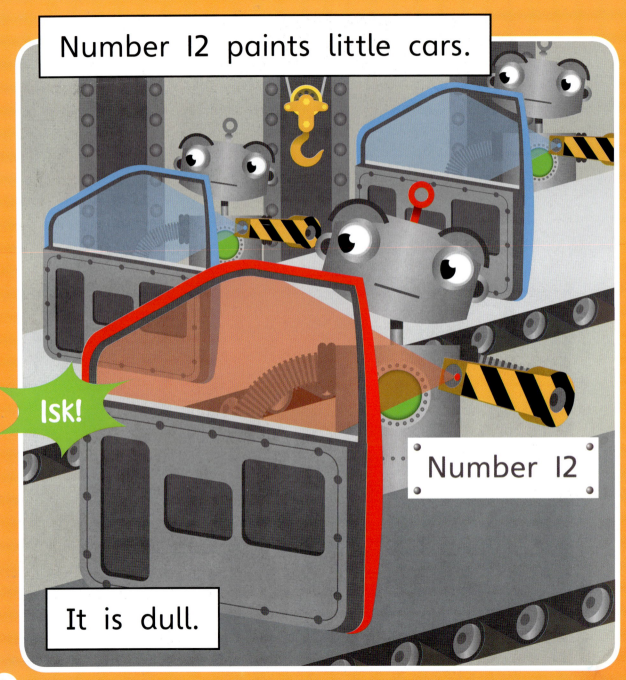

He paints some cars red.

He paints some cars green.

He paints some sports cars.

He paints some posh cars.

One night, Number 12 sees a film he likes.

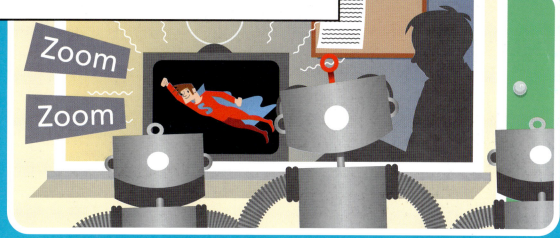

He comes up with a plan.

Zip Zap Man sets off the car alarm.

The cops come and get the robber.

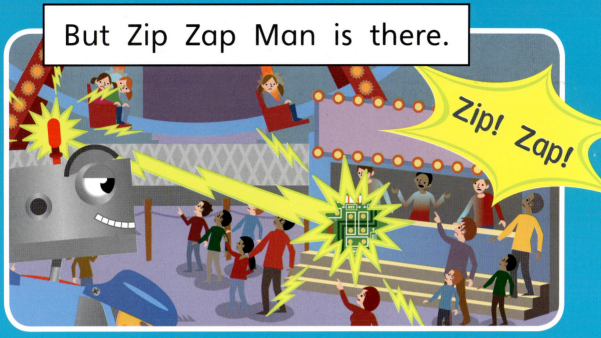

But Zip Zap Man is there.

The kids can get down.

Then he turns back into Number 12.

Bill has not seen him go.

The next morning, Number 12 is painting cars again. It is dull.

But what have the men seen?

No one thinks that Number 12 is Zip Zap Man.

He still paints cars. It is still dull. But at night, Number 12 is Zip Zap Man!

Zip! Zap!

That is the best job of all!